Rocky Mountain Elk

PORTFOLIO

FARCOUNTRY
PRESS

PHOTOGRAPHY OF DONALD M. JONES

Dedication

To my big brother Greg, for putting the first camera in my hands and for opening my eyes and heart for all that nature has to offer. I am forever indebted.

FRONT COVER: Large herd bull, with head held high and eyes forward, crests a small knoll in search of cows.

TITLE PAGE: Bull and cow pause in an open meadow.

RIGHT: A large bull steps out from a spruce forest and announces his presence with a loud bellow.

References used:
Elk Country, Dr. Valerius Geist. NorthWord Press, 1991.

North American Elk: Ecology and Management, Dale E. Toweil and Jack Ward Thomas. Smithsonian Institute Press, 2002.

ISBN 1-56037-306-7
Photography © 2004 by Donald M. Jones
© 2004 Farcountry Press

For more information about our books write Farcountry Press, P.O. Box 5630, Helena, MT 59604; call (800) 821-3874; or visit www.farcountrypress.com.

Created, produced, and designed in the United States.
Printed in Korea.

Bugling can be heard as early as the middle of August and as late as December.

INTRODUCTION

by Donald M. Jones

In the summer of 1985, I had the good fortune of being hired as a seasonal worker with the U.S. Forest Service. It was a busy fire year, and I found myself away from home a lot that season. The days were long, but the money was good. Before I knew it the summer was over, and I found myself in the unusual situation of having something besides lint in my pocket: I had cash! Having spent the previous seven years as a starving student, I had sold all of my camera equipment to make ends meet, the last piece bartered for a pair of boots. Suddenly, there I stood with enough money to dive back into what I loved: photography.

Before long, I had enough basic equipment—camera, tripod, and telephoto lens—to pursue my lifelong dream of becoming a wildlife photographer. To say that I was a little naive about the business of photography would be an understatement. Rather than participating in workshops or continuing education courses or even buying books, I just ventured out into the woods and took photos of whatever pleased me. Looking back I think it was my ignorance of the business that gave me the freedom to pursue my passion for the outdoors, specifically wildlife.

I think if someone had sat me down and explained to me just how difficult it was to break into wildlife photography, I probably would have hung up the cameras again. Thankfully, I blindly forged ahead, testing the market and developing my eye, always searching for the next great photograph.

Bull and harem feeding near the Cavel Range of western Alberta.

What started as a hobby grew to be a rather demanding part-time job. So, with the blessing of my wife Tess and our two boys, on August 4, 1994, I quit my day job; to this day I have not looked back. As I sit here writing this piece on my laptop, nearly 100,000 snow geese are flying overhead, traveling north along the Rocky Mountain Front—this is just one of my many offices. I still need to pinch myself from time to time just to be sure it's not all just a dream.

So why am I doing a book of elk photographs? I tell people that while I've photographed North American subjects ranging from musk oxen to crocodiles to elephant seals to polar bears, out of all my subjects elk are what I have photographed the longest and most consistently. Over the past eighteen years, I have witnessed—and, with luck, captured on film—elk exhibiting their behaviors in a wide variety of habitats, weather, and lighting. Though this book contains numerous never-before-seen images, it also contains some of my favorite and most-prized photographs, which have been published in magazines, calendars, and books.

Pulling images for this book was an easy enough task; narrowing it down to about 140 images was a killer. So many of these photographs have so much more meaning for me than what you as a reader will be able to see—be it the extreme cold and wind felt on my face while I watched a wolf chase a cow elk; or the sight of flying rocks and upturned earth and the sound of clashing antlers as two bulls fought it out; or the peace and tranquility I experienced while I sat near several slumbering bulls. We have chosen those images that we think will make you pause on the page, taking in the moment, while eagerly anticipating what is on the next. I hope we will be successful in that endeavor. As we scoured the massive collection and chose photographs for this collection, we tried to select shots that had at least two or more things going for it besides sharpness and proper exposure. Maybe it was the rolling of the eyes combined with the raising of the hoof, or possibly the clash of two bulls with muscles rippling and dust rising through their tangled antlers. Or perhaps the simplicity of the image made it special, such as a silhouetted bull against a sunrise or a newborn calf finding solace in a bed of grass.

I hope you will find this collection of my eighteen years of elk photography to be worthy of a place in your home. For those who find enjoyment in photographing elk, I hope you find inspiration, even if it's "I can do better." For those of you who enjoy the challenge of the hunt, I hope you, too, find inspiration—that the big one is still out there. And for all of those who pick up this book because of their fascination with and love for the Rocky Mountain elk, enjoy the images that follow and be grateful that we have such a magnificent creature living among us.

FACING PAGE: This bull was a favorite of mine from the early 1990s. We nicknamed him "Sylvester" because he dwarfed all other bulls. Rumor had it that he was finally killed by another bull. If true, I certainly would have liked to have seen his opponent.

ABOVE: A bull's upper canine teeth carry such names as buglers, whistlers, tushes, and tusks but are most commonly called ivories.

LEFT: Bull and small harem on a grassy hillside in the Mission Valley of Montana.

It's early August and this bull shows off the effects of good forage and health in the symmetry of his antlers and the sleekness of his coat.

LEFT: *A spike bull wades a glaciated river. Bulls in their second year will sport these single-tined antlers.*

BELOW: *Cow nuzzling her newborn calf. In its first week or so of life, the calf will be left in hiding most of the day, with the cow returning four to five times a day to nurse.*

11

Fresh out of the wallow, this bull, eyes bulging, runs through the brush in an attempt to herd his scattered cows.

Though it looks to be a family portrait, it isn't. Bulls offer nothing in the rearing of the young and will only seek out the females during the fall rutting period.

ABOVE: Two spike bulls are silhouetted on an open hillside. Spikes are generally the last of the bulls to lose their antlers, sometime carrying them through April.

RIGHT: Large herd of wintering elk feeding along the front range of the Rocky Mountains.

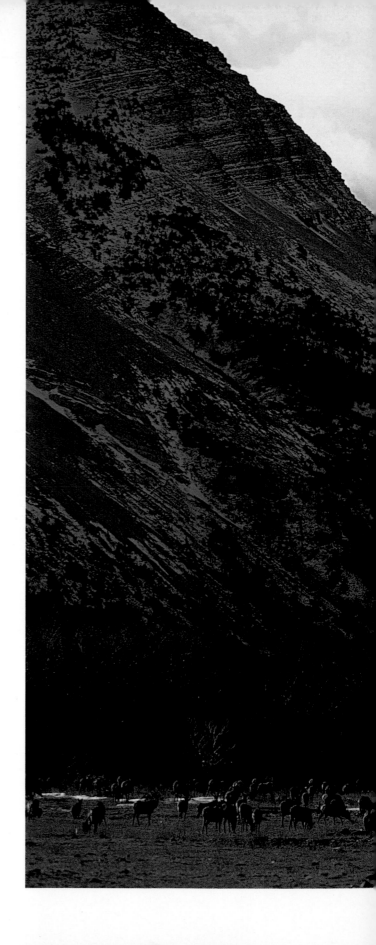

RIGHT: A bull stands and watches as a cow makes her way through the thick timber away from his harem.

BELOW: Because there are always marauding bulls and wandering cows to keep his eyes on, a bull bedding with his harem finds little rest.

FACING PAGE: Having fended off three smaller bulls that had attempted to scatter his harem, a bull emerges victoriously from an aspen stand. By late afternoon his harem number is cut in half, perhaps by other cunning bulls or because cows that have already bred have left the group.

This is the most intense fight I have ever witnessed. These bulls fought hard for approximately twenty minutes. Both bulls survived, though one walked away with a memento of the battle: a 3-inch piece of tine lodged in the back of his head.

Feeding along a pond in late summer, this bull carries two hitchhikers on its velvety headpiece.

LEFT: *Conspicuous imprints of elk.*

BELOW: *This calf finds comfort by lying on a river sand-bar and allowing the open breeze to whisk away the annoying insects.*

ABOVE: Rising from his bed, a bull shakes off the morning rain like a wet dog.

LEFT: Magnificent bull emerging from a curtain of old-growth spruce.

ABOVE: *With a dramatic facial expression, this 800-pound-plus bull lies down with a thud.*

RIGHT: *After the rut, bulls will distance themselves from the cows and form bachelor groups, like these nine bulls in Yellowstone National Park.*

LEFT: Though elk calves look to be all legs, this one appears particularly giraffe-like.

FACING PAGE: This bull, which had a bugle that sounded like Godzilla, frequented the same rutting area for about four years straight. Here, he's sporting the Whoopi Goldberg look.

This bull in the northern Rockies has made it through another winter and is just a few weeks from dropping his antlers.

ABOVE AND RIGHT: *I spent three days filming this old lone bull in December. On the fourth day I could only find tracks; they led to his carcass. During the night, seven wolves had taken him down. Two months later, I returned to the site of his demise, now under two feet of snow and ice.*

This rutting bull seems to rely more on attracting a female through noise and smell than actually searching for a female in estrus. Bugling generally silences any nearby competitors unless they are willing to challenge.

LEFT: *It's a cool October day and a calf finds himself being groomed by his mother, much like he has since his birth in late May or early June.*

BELOW: *Responding to a challenger's bugle, a bull leaves his cows and searches for his adversary.*

ABOVE: With ears pointed forward, a bedded bull listens to a distant bugle. In this case, distance is key; the opposing bugle is too far off to cause him to rise to his feet.

RIGHT: Sunrise captures this lone bull in a dramatic silhouette.

RIGHT: Like father like son—this calf takes to a young spruce as if in an apprentice program.

BELOW: A brown-headed cowbird finds a perch of velvet while hunting for insects around a sleeping bull.

Two mature bulls standing this close at this time of year usually means trouble for at least one of them. We nicknamed the bull on the left "Mr. Nasty"—he seems to have a greater distaste for humans with cameras than he does for other bulls. A number of us photographers have found "Mr. Nasty" on our heals at one time or another.

RIGHT: This bull carefully keeps me in sight as he digs through snow in search of grass.

BELOW: Half a dozen bulls feed in an open meadow. Though bulls gather and tolerate each other during the winter months, there still seems to be a hierarchy or pecking order if one bull gets too close to another.

FACING PAGE: A herd bull is dwarfed as he crosses a wide, slow-moving river.

Spring in the northern Rocky Mountains finds this bull with new antler growth as well as new grasses and forbs sprouting at his feet.

Not to be confused with being rude, this bull is signaling his intentions to a cow. If the cow lowers her head and twists it side to side and opens and closes her mouth, it's her "I've got a headache" signal to the bull.

This velvet-antlered bull lets out a yawn into the smoke-laden air as he wanders near a raging wildfire.

ABOVE: Like all children, this calf can't resist an opportunity for a roll in the mud.

LEFT: Elk herd feeding along a golden hillside at first light.

41

RIGHT: Two mature bulls find comfort in the tall grass on a hot August afternoon. In the coming weeks, these bulls will shed their velvet and leave their bachelor groups; they'll rejoin in late fall or early winter.

BELOW: A longe bull pauses and bugles along the banks of a river in the northern Rockies.

FACING PAGE: Evidence has shown that the volume of a bull's bugle is critical; the louder the call, the greater the distance the advertisement will travel.

Mature bull wandering through his domain.

Calves grow rapidly during their first year, sometimes reaching 300 pounds by the following spring.

ABOVE: *Three old bulls rest on a foggy ridge in late November.*

LEFT: *Bull working his way through a recently burned area. Prescribed burning can substantially increase forage conditions for elk as well as many other ungulate species.*

ABOVE: In winter, elk will often move into timbered areas where snow may be softer and forbs and browse are more accessible.

RIGHT: Nineteen wintering bulls pause on the sandy shoreline of a river as if in a quandary as to their next move.

ABOVE: *A bull, cow, and calf find refuge in an open meadow. The calf (center) displays unique white patches that she will carry throughout her life.*

FACING PAGE: *This bull has seen better days. I watched this old bull try to maintain a herd, but day after day he would lose his cows to younger, healthier bulls.*

RIGHT: Sporting a new crown of velvet, a bull peaks out from behind small spruce trees.

BELOW: Bulls will often place an object—stump, tree, rock, etc.—between themselves and an adversary when fighting, giving an almost comical look to their joust.

FAR RIGHT: As an impending storm looms to the west, a cow and calf, knee deep in a river, pause to survey their surroundings.

A bull drinks from a river while a cow wades to her belly in the cool water.

This younger bull acts as a satellite bull, keeping his distance from the herd so as not to be detected by the herd bull.

Here is a case in which still photography gives you more leverage than video. I sat with this bull for some time, hoping I could photograph him bugling against the golden backdrop. The best I came up with was this yawning image—it works!

ABOVE: *Two cows and a calf run through the river as a bull tries to herd them to the other side.*

RIGHT: *This cow pauses from feeding and rotates her ears like radars, surveying for danger.*

ABOVE: Bull showing off his lighter colored, thicker winter coat. During the spring his coat will become sleek and red.

LEFT: Cows are more likely to be found in large groups, lending to better security rather than better food. This is generally the opposite with bulls.

ABOVE: Two cows rear up on their hind legs and box it out. It is the front hooves that are most commonly used when competing for food or dominance.

LEFT: A bull lets out a bugle in the last of the evening light. While mid-day heat keeps the rutting activity to a minimum, the evening and nighttime temperatures will kick things into high gear.

ABOVE: *A two-week-old calf stretches his neck as his mother approaches. At birth, elk calves usually weigh between thirty and forty-five pounds.*

RIGHT: *This old bull with a bad limp makes his way to the river as if he is entering a therapeutic whirlpool—you can almost hear him sigh.*

Antlers serve as rank indicators and therefore are important in establishing dominance among males. These antlers belong to an old bull and have seven points (tines) each.

This is one of my favorite bugling images. Sometimes, when you are shooting, you just know you've captured something special—this was one of those cases.

RIGHT: *This bull has the look of "dear, please, not in front of the guys." This is one of my favorite elk pair images, representing both beauty and sensitivity.*

BELOW: *Calves will form small groups in which they sleep and play together; the mothers are never too far away, however, and are quick to respond if danger approaches.*

This bull is quick to cut off the escape route of a couple of his cows by heading them off and herding them back toward the remaining cows bedded on the riverbank.

Lone bull in late winter feeding at the edge of a spruce bog in the northern Rockies.

ABOVE: *A large herd of cows and calves feed in a snow-free meadow.*

FACING PAGE: *This bull will need a much larger tree if he has any hopes of succeeding at hide and seek.*

These two bulls fought hard and eventually found themselves up to their necks in the river. At times their heads were completely submerged, giving the impression that their antlers were locked—in fact it was more likely that one or the other simply refused to give up.

LEFT: Calf peering out from behind his mother on a frigid December morning.

BELOW: Bull and harem making their way along a bare mountain ridge in early September.

ABOVE: Week-old calf. Cow elk generally have just one calf per pregnancy, with twins only occurring in less than one-third of one percent of all pregnancies.

RIGHT: It's late June and this bull is showing just remnants of his winter coat while already sporting nearly half of his new antler growth for the year.

It's mid-October and more than likely all of these cows have bred,
yet this bull goes through the routine of checking each one of them.
Unless one of the cows is in estrus, this bull will likely spend little
energy trying to herd these cows.

After I photographed this bedded bull, a wolf started to howl about 100 yards away. The bull turned his head sharply to the right and stared hard in the direction of the wolf for a couple of minutes. The bull then turned his head back and continued to chew his cud. Is there a communication that's understood between prey and predator?

ABOVE: *One of my earliest elk images from Yellowstone National Park in 1986.*

FACING PAGE: *Weather always seems to be in flux during the elk rut. Here, a large bull lets out a bellow during an early-October snowstorm.*

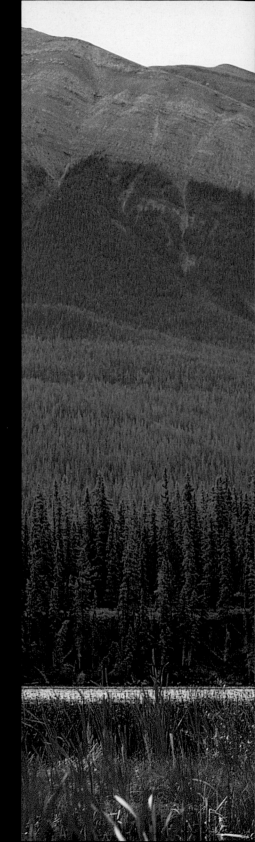

ABOVE: *Lazy days of summer. This bull can't afford not to be lazy—it takes a lot of forage to keep up with his metabolism and, therefore, he should be getting plenty of rest between feedings.*

RIGHT: *It's mid-August and this bull begins the quick process of stripping his velvet—it generally takes about twenty-four hours from beginning to end.*

It's truly amazing how these giant beasts can move through the forest with hardly a crack of a twig. Watching a bull twist and turn his head to maneuver his rack through the trees, you'd think he had built in sensors on his tines.

LEFT: One of the more majestic views of a bull with head raised back and moving directly away. You often hear hunters describe bulls that can reach back and scratch their rears with their antlers—I think they are often witnessing elk from this angle.

BELOW: A western beauty, a satellite bull makes his way across a meadow as storm clouds lift from a Rocky Mountain backdrop.

This bull is desperately trying to take control of his wandering harem as they attempt to flee across a rushing river.

RIGHT: It's hard to believe sometimes that one day this little calf might grow into a half-ton bull.

BELOW: Summer arrives and elk take to the higher meadows of western Montana in search of new grasses and forbs.

This bull's routine will change dramatically now that he has shed his velvet and the rut is just weeks away.

ABOVE: *I photographed this approaching bull and then quickly snatched up my twenty-five pounds of camera gear and ran. You don't have to have antlers on your head to be contested by these big fellows.*

LEFT: *A bull with an injured front left leg slowly negotiates a swift river during an early snowfall. His rutting days, at least for this year, are probably over, but his biggest hurdle is still to come as the hard days of a northern winter lie ahead.*

ABOVE: *Two cows run through a meadow with all the grace of a pair of show horses.*

RIGHT: *With temperatures at 25 degrees below zero, this bull is trying to expend as little energy as possible while bedded in a short-lived sunbeam.*

ABOVE: *Several cows feeding on underwater vegetation in western Montana. They look more like a band of moose than elk.*

LEFT: *These are the same bulls pictured fighting on page 70. The bull on the left pushed the bull on the right (larger one) backward up the bank until it looked like the latter's back would break. At that point the larger bull turned to leave—but not before the other bull got in one last jab of his antlers.*

LEFT AND BELOW: *Elk graffiti, the term often used for the chew marks left after an elk takes a bite out of aspen bark. The consumption of aspen bark takes place more often in the winter, when grasses and forbs are scarce.*

FACING PAGE: *With eyes bloodshot from lack of sleep, a bull lets out a bugle in response to a distant call. The rut is waning down and the bulls' bodies are starting to show the results: exhaustion, loss of weight, broken antlers, and, in some cases, broken bones.*

LEFT: Two bulls fight with an aspen tree between them. Earlier, these same two bulls had a dead tree between them when suddenly one of the bull's antlers took hold of the dead tree and pulled it out of the ground. It became stuck in the bull's antlers and he began to swing it around like a baseball bat, thoroughly baffling his opponent.

BELOW: Bull crossing a tributary in the northern Rockies.

Facing page: This bull appears not to know what to make of the two-legged photographer standing in front of him.

As his cows rest, this bull stands alert and on guard against escaping cows and roving bulls.

Four bachelor bulls lazily feed on grasses and wild rose leaves on an early-August morning.

RIGHT: *There's always a clown in the group!*

BELOW: *This bull leans over his cow as if to say, "It's time to go, dear." Little does he know that she has just been darted with a tranquilizer by a park service biologist. After the biologist collects his data, the cow will play catch up with the herd.*

FAR RIGHT: *It's early March in the Rockies and the snow is receding and the ice is melting—very soon this bull can hang up his head gear for another season.*

RIGHT: Why is this cow allowing this spike bull to nurse? Perhaps the question is better suited for a psychologist: he was not held enough as a calf, didn't know his father, etc.

BELOW: Rastafarian bull! Unlike its cousins the white-tailed and mule deer, which have a long period of time between shedding velvet and the rut, elk start the rutting period right away.

FACING PAGE: A bull stands at the forest edge and expels his breath on a frigid fall morning giving the appearance of a dragon before battle.

ABOVE: *What is often captioned in photos as bugling is actually the act of "flehmen" or lip-curling. This is a behavior in which males test the female urine using the vomeronasal organ in the palate to determine reproductive status.*

RIGHT: *Bull feeding in early June along a swift river.*

Winters in the northern Rockies are trying, and this bull has survived many.

ABOVE: *Ungulates, like this elk calf, grow rapidly during there first year for two important reasons: to gain size and strength to survive postnatal predation and to be strong enough to survive their first winter.*

FACING PAGE: *This is one of eight bulls I found and filmed within an aspen stand one morning. The woods sounded like a concert, with bulls bugling in every direction. Within thirty-five minutes I witnessed eight different fights all within thirty to forty yards from where I stood. It was an awesome adrenaline rush!*

ABOVE: *Herd of wintering cows running through an open field in the Gardiner Valley north of Yellowstone National Park.*

FACING PAGE: *Two bulls find shelter in an aspen stand. Though bulls will regroup after the rut, there still seems to be a pecking order in place. Often I have seen bulls show their canine teeth to opposing bulls who are impeding on their space.*

RIGHT: *Three bulls enjoying a siesta. Within a month, these group siestas will be replaced with bugling, fighting, and very little sleep.*

BELOW: *It's late October and a rather gaunt bull walks slowly up a hillside; the snow-blanketed mountains warn of the coming season.*

FACING PAGE: *Here, a large bull shows a bleeding wound to his left rib cage. On average, a rutting bull annually will receive thirty to fifty wounds. Most of the wounds are to the neck, shoulder, and rear regions.*

LEFT: *A bull wallows along the muddy banks of a river; wallowing is done mostly by older bulls.*

BELOW: *This bull lying in a meadow on a hot mid-August afternoon shows off his hardened, yet still velvet-covered, antlers.*

As if pretending to be a Lipizzaner stallion, this bull postures and approaches some cows, hoping to entice them to move in the direction he wishes.

RIGHT: A freshly cast antler. I saw a bull carrying this antler atop his head the evening before. Timing of antler shedding is primarily based on age and health. More sexually active prime bulls will cast their antlers before younger, less-active bulls.

BELOW: Both winter range and the routes the elk use to reach it are becoming increasingly scarce due to overdevelopment and intensive agriculture and livestock expansion.

A young bull lets out a bugle as he crosses a small stream during an early snowfall.

RIGHT: This bull is rubbing a young spruce as a symbol of dominance. It is said that only very confident bulls rub trees and this is their way of stating that they are willing to fight.

BELOW: A bull rises from his wallow covered in urine-soaked mud. Bulls will cover themselves with this pungent paste in order to better advertise to the awaiting females.

Two bulls take their battle to the river. Full-blown fights between herd bulls are rare. The brief, two-minute battle between these two bulls started on the riverbank and ended up in the river. The victor was the bull on the right; the loser was the challenger.

It's nearly sundown as this bull looks eastward toward the Mission Mountains of western Montana.